DIRT BIKE CRAZY

HONDA DIRT BIKES

By R. L. Van

Kaleidoscope
Minneapolis, MN

The Quest for Discovery Never Ends

···

This edition is co-published by agreement between Kaleidoscope and World Book, Inc.

Kaleidoscope Publishing, Inc.
6012 Blue Circle Drive
Minnetonka, MN 55343 U.S.A.

World Book, Inc.
180 North LaSalle St., Suite 900
Chicago IL 60601 U.S.A.

All rights reserved. No part of this book may be reproduced in any form without written permission from the publishers.

Kaleidoscope ISBNs
978-1-64519-091-2 (library bound)
978-1-64494-151-5 (paperback)
978-1-64519-194-0 (ebook)

World Book ISBN
978-0-7166-4363-0 (library bound)

Library of Congress Control Number
2019939016

Text copyright ©2020 by Kaleidoscope Publishing, Inc. All-Star Sports, Bigfoot Books, and associated logos are trademarks and/or registered trademarks of Kaleidoscope Publishing, Inc.

Printed in the United States of America.

FIND ME IF YOU CAN!

Bigfoot lurks within one of the images in this book. It's up to you to find him!

TABLE OF CONTENTS

Chapter 1: Racing Red **4**

Chapter 2: Dreaming Big **10**

Chapter 3: Best of Both Worlds **16**

Chapter 4: Team Honda **22**

Beyond the Book 28
Research Ninja 29
Further Resources 30
Glossary 31
Index 32
Photo Credits 32
About the Author 32

CHAPTER 1

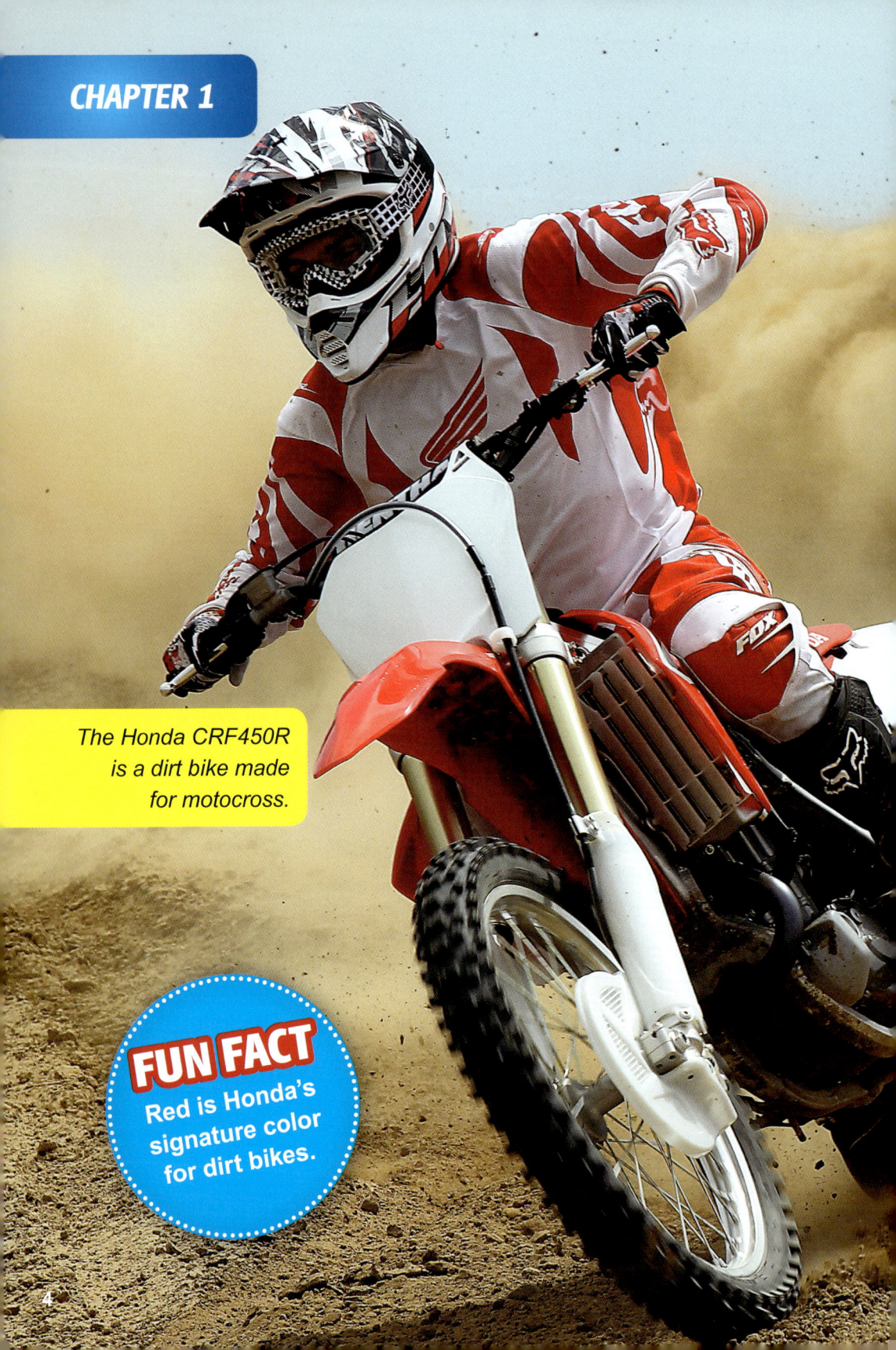

The Honda CRF450R is a dirt bike made for motocross.

FUN FACT
Red is Honda's signature color for dirt bikes.

Racing Red

Hudson straps on his boots. The sun beats down. He lowers the visor on his helmet. It helps block the sun. It also keeps dirt out of his eyes. Hudson climbs onto his Honda CRF450R.

Most of the bike is red. That's Hudson's favorite color. The **fenders** and seat have white accents. Hudson likes the gold forks. They stand out. The **fork guards** on the front wheel are red. They add a pop of color.

The race is about to start. Hudson has been racing **motocross** for a long time. He hopes to go pro someday. He'd like to join Team Honda. He wants to learn from racers like Ken Roczen.

Hudson pushes the electric start button. It's next to his handlebar. Hudson has the same bike as Roczen. But Roczen doesn't have an electric start. It adds 5 pounds (2.3 kg). The weight can slow riders down. But Hudson likes his electric start. It's easy to use.

Honda's CRF450R has something called launch control. It has three different modes. Hudson wants to choose the best one. The dirt on the track is dry. He presses the start button once. This chooses level one. The engine spins fastest on that level. A purple light blinks once. This means level one. The number of blinks tells Hudson the level.

Motocross tracks include obstacles like hills.

PARTS OF A
HONDA CRF450R

The gate drops. He releases the **clutch**. His bike speeds forward. The launch control gives him a boost. He starts out ahead of the other racers. He rides over a high jump. Hudson lands hard on the dirt. It doesn't bother him. The CRF450R has springs to absorb the shock. They're in the forks and under the seat. His ride stays smooth.

Hudson zooms along the track. He takes a sharp turn. He knows his Honda will carry him to victory.

Springs help absorb the impact from landing jumps.

CHAPTER 2

Dreaming Big

Soichiro Honda was known for standing out. He wore patterned suits and colorful shirts. He wanted to be on the factory floor with his workers. Honda brought this spirit to his company. He wanted Honda products to stand out, too.

Honda grew up in Japan. He started his career as a mechanic. But he wanted to do more than just fix things. He wanted to make them.

The D-Type was the first motorcycle made by Honda.

He started attaching small engines to bikes. Honda turned this into a new company. That was in 1948. It was called Honda Motor Company. Honda and his business partner had a dream. They wanted to make the world's best motorcycles. Honda released the "Dream" D-Type motorcycle in 1949. It stood out. Most motorcycles on the road were black. Honda's was maroon.

But Honda wanted to do something big. He wanted to win a race. The Isle of Man Tourist Trophy race was perfect. No one had ever entered on a Japanese bike.

Honda sent a team to race in 1959. The team studied the track. They wanted to do well. The Isle of Man is an island between England and Ireland. It was a long trip from Japan. The riders had six connecting flights. When they arrived, their bikes had become rusty. And they had been studying the track using an old map! But they didn't let it stop them. They didn't win. But people were interested in the new brand.

Honda's dream came true in 1961. Honda racers returned to the Isle of Man. A Honda racer won the lightweight category. Honda continued to have good luck that year. An Australian rider named Tom Phillis made history. He rode a Honda in the world championship. He rode it to victory. It was Honda's first world championship win.

FUN FACT
The top five riders in the 1961 Tourist Trophy lightweight category all rode Hondas!

Mike Hailwood won the 1961 Isle of Man Tourist Trophy lightweight category on a Honda. His average speed was 88.23 miles per hour (141.99 km/h).

Honda sold its millionth motorcycle in the United States in 1968.

Honda motorcycles became popular in the United States. Honda changed people's opinions about motorcycles. Honda motorcycles were available to everyone. They were fun and easy to ride. They were advertised to both men and women. Honda bikes were less expensive than others. More people could afford them. Many new people bought motorcycles. Honda changed the motorcycle industry in the United States.

EVERYTHING HONDA

Honda makes more than just motorcycles and dirt bikes. Honda makes lawn mowers, cars, and race cars. Honda makes airplanes. Honda has even made a robot. ASIMO was built in 2000. He was built to help people with disabilities. He can carry things. He can go up and down stairs. He can run and jump. He can also play soccer.

FUN FACT
The Honda Super Cub was introduced in 1958. Its front cover blocked the wind from lifting women's skirts.

CHAPTER 3

Best of Both Worlds

Maryam and Evan both have Honda dirt bikes. They ride on trails together. Maryam likes exploring mountain trails. She also races motocross. Evan competes in rally races. Those take place in the desert. They're much longer than other races.

Maryam loves her bike. She rides a Honda CRF250RX. She thinks it's the best of both worlds. It's fast and light for motocross races. But it's smooth enough for off-road riding. It's based on the Honda CRF250R. That's one of Honda's racing bikes. But this one has off-road features. It holds more fuel. Its back wheel is smaller. This means the tire can be taller. It won't get pinched against rocks or logs as easily. Maryam is less likely to get a flat tire. The 250RX also has a kickstand. This makes it easy for Maryam to leave her bike if she wants to stop. She likes to wade in streams and skip rocks on lakes.

The Honda CRF250RX is a good choice for riders who like off-road and motocross.

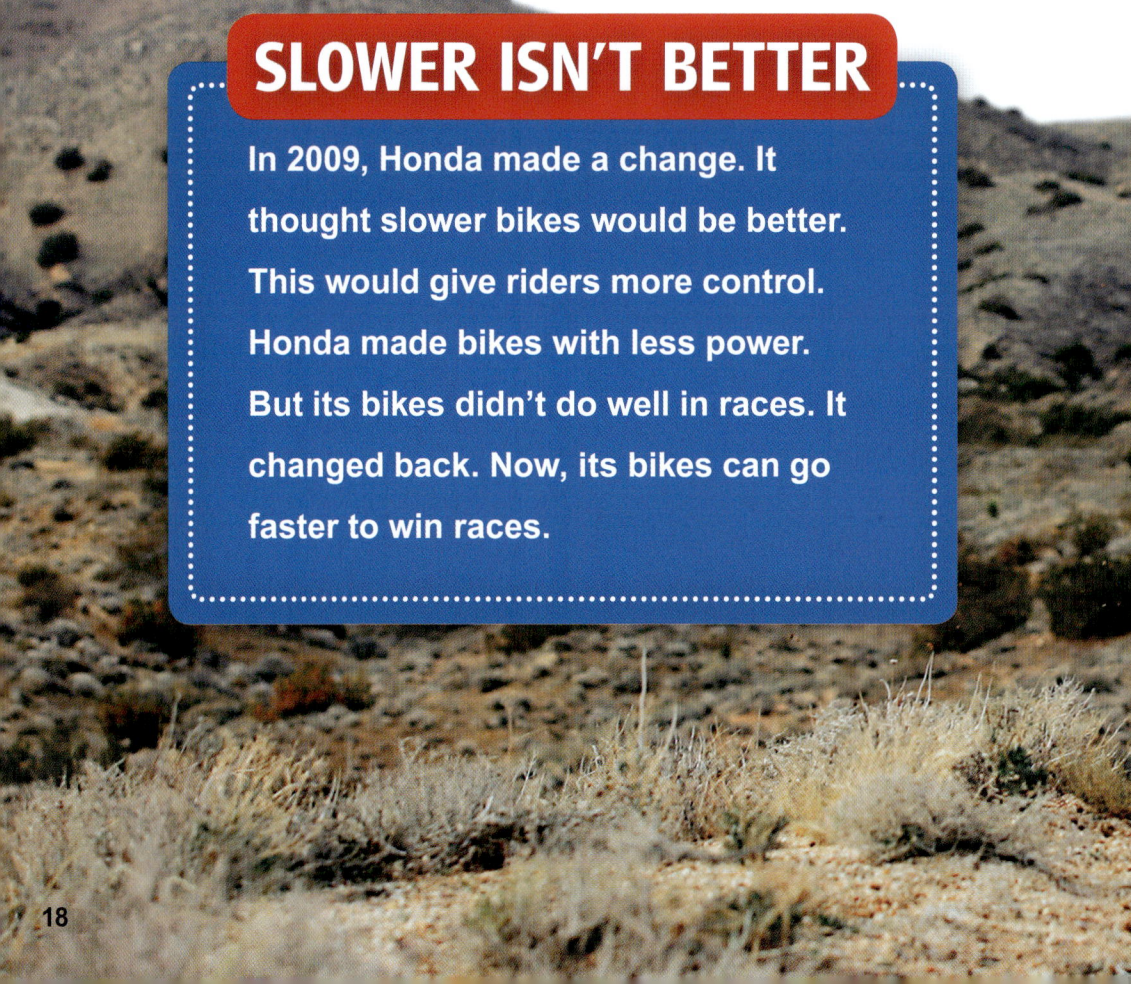

The 250RX has softer **suspension** than the 250R. It's not as stiff. This is better for trail rides. Maryam can go over logs and rocks. The bike rides smoothly instead of bouncing around. But it's still stiffer than other off-road bikes. This means it also works for racing.

Maryam and Evan will need to go home soon. But they want to test out each other's bikes. Evan rides a CRF450X. It's designed for cross-country riding. But it has more power than most off-road bikes. The CRF450X has won many rally races. Evan is glad he has a winning bike.

SLOWER ISN'T BETTER

In 2009, Honda made a change. It thought slower bikes would be better. This would give riders more control. Honda made bikes with less power. But its bikes didn't do well in races. It changed back. Now, its bikes can go faster to win races.

Some off-road riders compete in rallies, which can take place over many days.

FUN FACT
The Dakar Rally is a famous rally. It's over two weeks long.

Maryam notices that Evan's bike has only one **silencer**. Hers has two. But his bike is quieter than most bikes this size. She likes that Evan's bike has a six-speed **transmission**. It gives more gear options. Hers is a five-speed.

Maryam and Evan have fun trying out each other's bikes. They switch back to drive their own Hondas home.

BIKE MODEL	CRF450R	CRF450X	CRF250RX
SUITABLE FOR	Motocross	Off-road	Motocross/Off-road
ENGINE SIZE	450cc	450cc	250cc
TRANSMISSION	5-speed	6-speed	5-speed
WEIGHT	247 pounds (112 kg)	275 pounds (125 kg)	244 pounds (111 kg)
BASE PRICE	$9,299	$9,799	$8,299

COMPARE AND CONTRAST
HONDA DIRT BIKES

CRF450R

CRF450X

CRF250RX

CHAPTER 4

Ken Roczen has been racing for Honda since 2017.

Team Honda

Ken Roczen is a supercross rider. Supercross racing is done in a stadium or arena. Obstacles block the track. There are hills and **whoops**. There are jumps and sharp turns. A deep layer of mud and dirt covers the ground. Riders get stuck while they race.

It's January 2019. Roczen is waiting for the gate to drop. It's been a long time since his last race. He's been racing since he was three years old. But two years ago, he fell during a race. He broke his left arm. It took him almost a year to heal. He got back on his dirt bike. But he wasn't ready. He fell again. This time he hurt his right arm. Now, he's finally healed enough to race.

FUN FACT
Ken Roczen's racing number is 94.

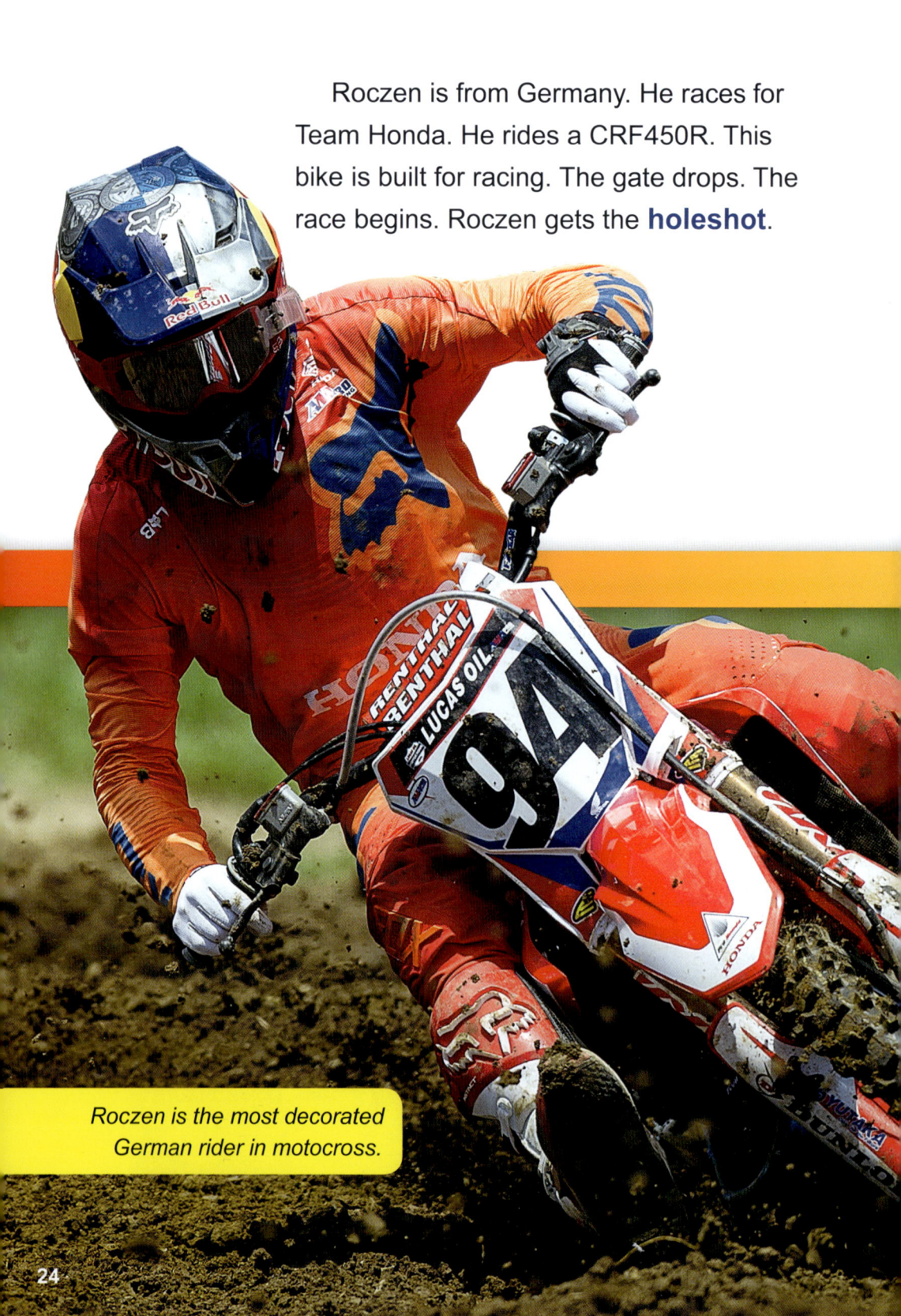

Roczen is from Germany. He races for Team Honda. He rides a CRF450R. This bike is built for racing. The gate drops. The race begins. Roczen gets the **holeshot**.

Roczen is the most decorated German rider in motocross.

It's thanks to his bike. Honda markets this bike's ability to get the lead. Roczen flies over hills. His bike powers through deep ruts. He comes in second place. It's not a bad way to start the season.

Trevor Stewart is another rider for Team Honda. Stewart races in Big 6 and WORCS competitions. These are both off-road races. But they're shorter than other off-road competitions. They're usually shorter than two hours.

FUN FACT
Roczen's favorite food is pizza.

The CRF450RX is a great choice for off-road riders like Trevor Stewart.

Stewart rode for fun when he was younger. He drove off-road with his dad and his brother. He tried motocross when he was fifteen. But he didn't like it as much. He wanted to do longer races on rougher ground. So he went back to his roots to race off-road. He rides a CRF450RX. It's a lot like Roczen's bike. But it has updates for off-road. The bike works well for Stewart.

Honda has been making motorcycles for decades. Its dirt bikes speed past the competition. Each year, Honda improves its dirt bike designs. Honda racers like Roczen and Stewart show off their bikes' abilities. They're proud to Ride Red.

BEYOND
THE BOOK

After reading the book, it's time to think about what you learned. Try the following exercises to jumpstart your ideas.

THINK

THAT'S NEWS TO ME. The book mentions a crash where Ken Roczen injured his left arm. How might news sources be able to fill in more detail about this? What new information could you find in news articles? Where could you go to find those sources?

CREATE

SHARPEN YOUR RESEARCH SKILLS. Honda builds more than just dirt bikes. It even built a robot called ASIMO. Where could you go in the library to find more information about ASIMO? Who could you talk to who might know more? Create a research plan. Write a paragraph about your next steps.

SHARE

WHAT'S YOUR OPINION? In the book, Maryam thought the CRF250RX was the best of both racing and off-road. Do you think the CRF250RX is the best of both worlds? Do you disagree? Use information from the text to support your answer. Share your position and evidence with a friend. Does your friend agree with you?

GROW

DRAWING CONNECTIONS. Honda started out building street motorcycles. Create a drawing that shows the connections between motorcycles and dirt bikes. What kinds of changes had to be made? How does learning about motorcycles help you better understand dirt bikes?

RESEARCH NINJA

Visit www.ninjaresearcher.com/0912 to learn how to take your research skills and book report writing to the next level!

RESEARCH

DIGITAL LITERACY TOOLS

SEARCH LIKE A PRO
Learn about how to use search engines to find useful websites.

FACT OR FAKE?
Discover how you can tell a trusted website from an untrustworthy resource.

TEXT DETECTIVE
Explore how to zero in on the information you need most.

SHOW YOUR WORK
Research responsibly— learn how to cite sources.

WRITE

GET TO THE POINT
Learn how to express your main ideas.

PLAN OF ATTACK
Learn prewriting exercises and create an outline.

DOWNLOADABLE REPORT FORMS

Further Resources

BOOKS

Lanier, Wendy Hinote. *Dirt Bikes.* Focus Readers, 2017.

Shaffer, Lindsay. *Motocross Cycles.* Bellwether Media, 2019.

Weston, Mark. *The Story of Car Engineer Soichiro Honda.* Lee & Low Books, 2018.

WEBSITES

Factsurfer.com gives you a safe, fun way to find more information.

1. Go to www.factsurfer.com.
2. Enter "Honda Dirt Bikes" into the search box and click 🔍.
3. Select your book cover to see a list of related websites.

Glossary

clutch: The clutch lets the rider change gears by stopping power from flowing to the engine. Once he was in gear, Hudson released the clutch and his bike shot forward.

fenders: Fenders are the pieces of a dirt bike that protect the front and back tires. The fenders on Honda dirt bikes are bright red.

fork guards: Fork guards are plastic pieces that protect the forks, which absorb shock from the road. The Honda CRF450R has red fork guards covering the forks.

holeshot: A holeshot is when someone gets the lead out of the gate in a motocross or other motorsport race. Ken Roczen used his bike's launch control to get the holeshot.

motocross: Motocross is a sport for racing dirt bikes or other motorcycles. Ken Roczen competes in supercross racing, which is a kind of motocross race.

silencer: The silencer on a bike lowers the amount of noise created by an engine. Some Honda dirt bikes have one silencer, while others have two.

suspension: A vehicle's suspension protects it from bumps and makes the ride feel smoother. Honda dirt bikes have springs in the forks and under the seat for better suspension.

transmission: A vehicle's transmission allows it to change gears. The transmission in Stewart's bike changes gears so it can go faster up the hill.

whoops: Whoops are a series of small hills on a motocross or supercross track. The suspension on Maryam's bike helps her drive over whoops quickly.

Index

ASIMO, 15

CRF250R, 16, 18
CRF250RX, 16–21
CRF450R, 5–9, 20–21, 23–25
CRF450X, 18–21

D-Type, 11

electric starters, 6–7

forks, 5, 8, 9

Honda, Soichiro, 10–12

Isle of Man Tourist Trophy, 12

launch control, 7–9

motocross, 5–9, 16–18, 20, 26

off-road races, 16–18, 20, 25–26

Phillis, Tom, 12

rally races, 16, 18, 19
red, 4, 5, 11, 27
Roczen, Ken, 5–6, 23–27

Stewart, Trevor, 25–27
supercross, 23–25
Super Cub, 15
suspension, 9, 16–18

Team Honda, 5, 23–27
transmission, 20

PHOTO CREDITS

The images in this book are reproduced through the courtesy of: Honda News, front cover, pp. 3, 4–5, 6–7, 7, 8, 9, 10–11, 14, 15 (top), 15 (bottom), 16, 17, 18–19, 21 (top), 21 (middle), 21 (bottom), 22–23, 23, 26–27, 30; AP Images, pp. 11, 12, 13; Red Line Editorial, pp. 20–21; Bryan Lynn/Icon Sportswire/AP Images, pp. 24–25.

ABOUT THE AUTHOR

R. L. Van is an editor and writer from Minnesota. She loves books, animals, and crossword puzzles.